Healing My Heart: Poems of Identity, Truth, and Transformation From Four Voices

Kelly Garnett Joseph-Brooks

LEGACY OF THREE PUBISHING

Text copyright @ Kelly Garnett Joseph-Brooks, 2025

ISBN: 978-1-7379027-3-7 (Paperback)

Any references to historical events, real people, or real places are used fictitiously. Names, characters, and places are products of the author's imagination.

Printed by Legacy of Three Publishing, LLC, in the United States of America
First printing edition 2025

Legacy of Three Publishing, LLC
P.O Box 852
Godley, Texas, 76044

www.kgjbrooks.com

Dedication

To Andre
the love of my life,
my steady anchor.

To Lori and Kristy,
the fire behind my words.

To Big Mike,
the son I was joyfully gifted.

To Jeremy,
my brother,
a fellow artist whose beats
echo my voice.

To the Garnetts,
my paternal family,
it's through your love—
I have gotten to know my father.

To my MACK,
Irish DeSilva,
through your love and encouragement—
I found the missing pieces.

To my siblings,
your love and admiration
pushes me forward.

Remember your love carries—
through every page,
every poem,
every dream

My Truth Begins Here

I was nine years old when truth shattered my world.
Arthur "June" Joseph Jr., the man I called Daddy,
was not my biological father.
My true father was Gary "Squeek" Garnett.
That revelation struck like a storm without warning.
In one instant, the ground beneath me cracked,
and the security of childhood slipped away.

Abandonment.
Identity.
Trust.

I buried them deep—along with the anger,
the pain, the questions with no answers.

But silence has weight,
and mine became too heavy to carry.

Years of therapy, prayer, and reflection brought me here.
Brought me to these poems.
They are fragments of my journey,
voices rising from the three adults who shaped my life—
my mother, my father, and my biological father.

Each left their mark.
Each gave me pieces of the woman I would become.

This book is testimony:
healing is possible,
and pain can be transformed into power.

It is also a warning,
to parents navigating brokenness
and the quiet ache of co-parenting.
Remember—your children stand at the center of truth.

Be bridges, not walls.
Unite, don't divide.

My truth,
my scars,
my voice—
is an offering:
laid bare so others may find
the courage to confront their own.

Table of Contents

Shattered Foundations   1

Disintegration   10

Family Alienation   11

Rewriting History   13

Angel   15

Cousin Julian   17

The Truth   19

Be Nice   20

Immaculate Conception   23

Question and Answer Session   24

Do You Want to See Him?   25

Deep Denial   26

Moving From New Orleans   28

Never Tell Them   30

Wasn't Their Place   31

Moving Forward   32

Pulling Away   34

Barbershop Encounter   36

School Visit   37

Mother-In-Law's Plan   38

Wedding Guest   39

Not My Real Daddy   42

Not His Decision   43

You Ain't Shit   44

Piecing Together My Identity   47

Forgiveness   49

The Death of My Father   50

Therapy   51

Finding Myself   52

Reconnection   55

Garnett Family Reunion   57

My Teedies   58

Acceptance   59

Full Circle   60

Healing My Heart   62

About the Author   65

Shattered Foundations

It was Saturday.
Excitement bubbled inside me—
my brothers and I,
the fearless Three Musketeers,
were going to spend the day
with our grandfather.

Now living with our grandparents,
we missed our parents terribly.
Especially Mom.

Mom was on a "vacation from reality,"
leaving Dad alone
to do what he always did—
work, in his extraordinary way.

We were too young
to understand Mom's absence
or why we couldn't stay with Dad.

So, the Three Musketeers—
and our newborn sister—
went to live "over the river."

Over the river—Avondale, Louisiana—
felt like a foreign country.

A world apart from the Crescent City.
Even the people seemed different.

Those months were confusing.
I struggled to connect
with our new environment—
unlike my siblings.
It wasn't for a lack of trying—
I just felt lost,
uninspired,
and sad.

Looking back,
I realize this was probably
my first brush with depression.

I couldn't express it—
not to my grandparents,
aunts,
or uncles.

I felt out of place,
drained by the effort to adapt.

School seemed welcoming,
but soon I realized why—
and I began to shut down even more.

The teachers were extra nice—
too nice—
because they "knew our situation."

I just wished I knew
what our situation was.

They whispered that we'd been abandoned—
four teachers, chatting in the hall.

Their words cut deep,
because it wasn't true.

And I hated being pitied.
I fit in better before and after school—
waiting for the bus, riding it, walking home.

Inside the school walls, every day was torture.
I felt inept. Invisible. Lost.

Migraines pounded my head.
I wished my parents could pull me
from the vortex of confusion.

It drained the best of me,
shrinking me down to invisible.
Small.

We begged our grandmother
to let us go to New Orleans with our grandfather.
Backyard play had grown tiresome—
we longed for something more.

When she finally relented,
we were over the moon.
We were culturally New Orleans children,
trapped "over the river."

The difference was stark.
I couldn't explain it,
but my siblings and I all felt it.

They navigated it easily;
I languished.

The thought of roaming the 7th Ward
filled my heart with joy.

Going home—even without seeing our parents—
felt grounding, inspiring, freeing.

Our world, our streets, our laughter.
Heat and humidity? We barely noticed.
Children who loved to run outside,
wild, and free.

Just an ordinary Saturday—yet unforgettable.
A storm approached,
but we were too distracted by laughter,
too lost in joy,
to notice that in mere seconds,
everything would change.

My grandfather owned a barbershop.
He often peeked outside to check on us.
But that day,
his body language was different—
a look I would never forget.

Urgency painted his face—
like he had seen something disturbing.
He bolted from the shop,
waving and yelling, desperate for attention.
I couldn't catch the words.
Suddenly, two men stopped.
My grandfather spoke with them.
We kept playing tag,
laughing and giggling, oblivious.

We paid it no mind—
grown-ups' business, not ours.
Then he called us,
motioning toward him and the two strangers.

The Three Musketeers started walking,
hands entwined with our little brother's.

He told us to leave our little brother
and for T— and me to come forward.
Mom always taught us to care for each other—
so we disobeyed
and walked toward him and the strangers.

Though I was only nine,
I had an unusual ability to read people.
One of the strangers looked uneasy.

He looked annoyed—
a silent let's just get this over with—
while his companion appeared warm and welcoming.

As we reached arm's length, our grandfather blurted:
"Kelly and T—, this is your father—Squeek."

In that instant, an aha moment struck me.
Three things occurred simultaneously:
the realization itself,
letting go of our little brother's hand,
and T—'s reaction to the news.

The words swirled in my mind, over and over:
"Kelly and T—, this is your father—Squeek."

That aha moment became a revelation.
Suddenly, it all made sense—
the tension I had always felt
at Mom's family gatherings.

When T— and I entered, adults paused.
Children caused quiet, yes,
but this felt different—
an unusual energy when it was us.

Mom always seemed sad.
Dad looked frozen mid-verbal takedown.
Perhaps that explained the tension.
I could never have imagined
it had anything to do with our lineage.

T— cried like I had ever seen.
The news pierced him.
Screams tore from his chest.
I felt we could be swept away by his tears.

Between sobs, he repeated:
"June is my father!
Where is June!
I want my daddy!"

Raged collided with my revelation.
My beloved brother sobbed uncontrollably.
And the two strangers had already hurried past us.

I thought: How could our father just pass us by?
June—our real dad—would never do that.

Confusion surged.
Mom had always been honest…
hadn't she?

I needed Mom.
She was away—
taking that so called "vacation from reality."

Only she could explain
the revelation we'd just received
at nine, eight, and five.

We didn't doubt our grandfather,
but Mom had never told us
about another father.

Why keep it a secret?
Mom never kept secrets.

Our grandfather told us
to go back to play.
But for the first time,
we didn't want to.

Huddled against Grandpa's shop,
we whispered about the revelation.
T— insisted
Squeek wasn't our dad.
We laughed and agreed June was our father.
Case closed.
Returning to tag, we knew life had changed forever.

Back "over the river", our grandmother
waved us in. As always,
we brought our little brother.
Even after the revelation,
we clung to Mom's teaching:
care for each other.

Grandma opened a beautiful photo album—
a couple I'd never seen stared back.

She pointed to a woman in a white lace gown,
veil adorned with flowers,
standing beside a handsome man in a white tuxedo.

"Do you know them?" she asked.
We shook our heads.
"Do you know her?" Still no.
"This is your mom," she said.

Then: "Kelly and T—— this is your mom and dad."
T— blurted, "That man isn't June!"
We laughed.

We had agreed: June was our dad.
Respectfully, we declined to call Squeek our father.
We complimented Mom's beauty,
then left Grandma's room to play.

Huddled in our room,
we whispered about Mom's beauty.
The "Squeek situation" wouldn't fade—
not until we reunited with our parents,
Arthur (June) and Deborah Joseph.

Our visit with our grandparents stretched long.
No one could force us to acknowledge
someone who passed us on the street.

Again, we agreed:
June was our father—
hands down.

That aha moment reshaped our family.
Nearly five months would pass
before returning to our parents.

The damage? Already done.
An emptiness settled in,
a feeling of loss that seeped into my heart and soul.

I didn't cry that day,
but I did on others—
mourning the aha moment that changed my life.

Answers never satisfied.
A deep sense of loss lingered—
loss of trust in the adults around us,
especially Mom.

Without a word,
Mom forbade any mention of Squeek.
Cracks formed between us;
fissures rose to the surface.

I don't know when our family became a war zone,
but it did seem like it started
around the time of the "Squeek revelation."

June became distant from me and T—.
Mom became despondent.
Arguments erupted.
Our family—once happy—
seemed visibly wounded.

At nine, my brother at eight
and our little brother five,
we weren't ready for that aha moment.
It changed us—
in ways I still ache over,
even now at fifty-six.

On the streets, playing tag,
we learned the truth:
the man who had raised us all our lives
wasn't our father.

Looking back, even decades later,
the ache remains.
Loss.
Confusion.
The shift in our family dynamics—
it still lingers.

Yet, through it all, resilience shines:
we survived,
we loved,
and we held one another close.

Shattered foundations, yes.
But beneath the cracks,
the Three Musketeers—my brothers and I—
learned to rebuild,
to navigate the complexities of love, truth, and family.

Disintegration

Right before my eyes,
my family unraveled—
the "aha moment"
detonating at the center.

My father was not my blood.
The revelation tore through us
like a tsunami colliding with a hurricane.

The devastation struck instantly.
The moment June was stripped of fatherhood,
my family began to splinter into shards.

My father withdrew from
me and my brother.
My mother sank deeper into silence—
her depression
a shadow over the house.

Tension thickened the air—
nothing would ever be the same.

Laughter gave way to screams,
love dissolved into pain.
A fracture opened wide—
we were no longer whole.

The disintegration of my foundation.
The collapse of my support.
The unraveling of my life.

Family Alienation

One side mocked us,
while the other side ostracized us,
but in the end,
both sides tried to rewrite history—
concerning our banishment from the family circle.

Too young to understand,
the why's and the how's—
just knew the pain
was sometimes unbearable.

I always wondered
what led to our exile—
never understood,
with many scenarios swirling in my head.

Although it hurt beyond
what I was able to articulate,
there was an anger
that propelled me forward.

I learned early on
that I had no village—
outside my parents and siblings.

I relied on no one
other than the family inside my home.
Going through daily stressors and heartache—
they alone stood with me—
always there to assist.

I dealt with this anger and loneliness
as best as I could.

The times I would become the angriest
were when family outside the circle would ask,
"Why aren't you coming to family functions?"

Back then, I wanted to say—
How do you attend an event you were never invited to?

Now, the me that has grown up
and redefined family
chuckles when I'm posed that question.

I would have answered with words,
but I believe my laughter was sufficient.

Through alienation,
I learned independence—
that family can fail you,
and how I respond
decides if I move forward
or stay trapped
in a cycle of pain and regret.

I chose going forward.

Rewriting History

When my family and I were ostracized—
cast out of the family circle—
a new narrative appeared.

They said:
"They just stopped coming around."
"They think they're too good for us."

That lie…
obscured the truth.
The real story?
We were kicked out—
like a bag of smelly trash.

The family historians—
(the self-appointed ones)—
devised a plan:
tell anyone and everyone
that we were being bougie,
that we thought
we were better than them.

To this day—
I still don't know the full reason
why we were exiled.

But I doubt any of those
family historians
would ever go on record
and tell the whole truth.

After years of
healing…
soul-searching…
grieving…

I learned firsthand:
Rewriting history
can distort legacies—
can erase people
while they're still alive.
But in rewriting my family history—
with my own voice,
my own truth—
I may have lost my village…
but I gained something greater:
independence,
And peace.

Angel

As a nine-year-old,
I had an encounter
with a heavenly being
living on earth.

She was beautiful and intelligent,
a smile that filled my heart,
and kindness that pierced my soul.

She was the apple of my eye,
offering me unconditional love
I had been missing
while my mother was away.

Her love sustained me,
pushed me forward,
and reminded me:
hope is ever-growing.

Ever-growing like an Australian apple berry—
a silky, twinning plant
with bell-shaped blooms.
She helped me to bloom.

Now, as a fifty-something woman,
I feel grateful and blessed
to have experienced a love
that few ever truly know.

I will never forget her kindness—
how she loved on three forlorn children,
longing for their mother's arms.

Her heavenly name was Angel.
But here on earth, she was called Elaine.

Peace.
Blessings.
Love.
My sweet Teedy Elaine—
what you gave me and my siblings
was more than you could ever imagine.

Cousin Julian

My brother comes running—
frantically searching—
and finds me.
He looks distraught.
He says,
"I just got jumped."

As his big sister,
I had to avenge this wrong.

I said,
"Take me to the perpetrators."

But T— says,
"Not necessary."
"Our cousin Julian helped him."

Now my mind
spins like a Rolodex.
Cousin Julian?
I don't remember
Cousin Julian

Then T— adds,
"He's Gary Garnett's nephew."

Gary Garnett—
our bio dad.

We called him that.
Or sometimes…
Squeek.

All this time we are talking,
I don't even notice—
Julian is standing right there.

I thank him
for helping T—.

He smiles and says:
"That's ok. We are family."
"Y'all will never have to worry about nothing."

That day,
Cousin Julian
made a deep impression on me.

The Truth

Fall of 1976,
my mother returned from the hospital.
My brother and I
had so many questions for her.

Who was Gary Garnett?
Was he T— and my father?
Why did she not tell us the truth?

Thinking back to that day,
my mother really handled the questioning well.
She was calm,
and very measured
with her answers.

She told us
she was married to Gary Garnett—
that he was T— and my father.

But she never answered
why she kept it a secret.
We never received an answer.

My brother and I
can only speculate.
My mother...
has taken that secret
to the grave.

So, yes—
we got the partial truth,
But it only felt like a small victory.

There were so many other questions—
and answers
we deserved
to have that day.

We never received
what was due to us—
the truth.

Be Nice

It was an exciting time—
my favorite aunt, Pretty, was getting married.
I couldn't wait to see my family,
especially my cousins Nessa and Little Pretty.
We were three peas in a pod.

As soon as we saw one another,
Little Pretty, Nessa and I went off to enjoy the wedding.
We are laughing and dancing,
sharing silly stories.

Suddenly,
we are interrupted
by an unwanted intruder.

He mutters, "I am your father."

I become visibly upset
and say nothing.

What do you say to a stranger?
As a child,
I was taught not to speak to strangers.
To me,
Gary Garnett was a stranger.

I roll my eyes,
run off with Nessa and Little Pretty
and look for my brother.

He would understand my anger.

Before I could tell him what happened,
T— said that
"Squeek was bothering him."
Squeek—
that was what we called our biological dad.

I don't know why.
But how would I know
to call him anything else?

He was a stranger to me.
And really…
I didn't care.

I didn't understand why he was at the wedding.

Once we were told about Gary Garnett,
he became a topic everyone
and anyone
would bring up
in our presence.

As I'm talking to my brother
the stranger walks up again.
He says,
"I am your father."

I'm so frustrated—
I blurt out:
"So."

My brother and I laughed
and run off.

My brother headed off
to play with our other cousins.
I headed off to tell my parents.
I said,
"The stranger was bothering my brother and me."
And I'm shocked
by what my father says:
"Be nice to him."

My mother becomes enraged.
They start arguing.
And I'm just standing there,
confused.

I wasn't ready
for my father's response:
"Be nice."

I think to myself:
I don't know him.
He is a stranger.
Why would I be nice?

Now I am madder at the stranger.
He's caused an argument between my parents.
He has caused confusion in me—
and he irritated me—
by pointing out he was my father.

I wonder—
is this when stranger danger became real?
Be nice, became a confusing request,
And the cracks in our family
became increasingly more visible.

Immaculate Conception

My mother was the greatest storyteller I knew.
Her stories were always captivating—
her tales alluring.
Never did I imagine
she would write me into her-story.

At sixteen,
she told me I was the product of "immaculate conception."
That meant Squeek was not my father.
This time her story did not captivate—
it shattered me.

I could feel the depth of her pain,
so deep that she created an unbelievable tale
to shield herself,
or perhaps to shield me.

I tried to brush it off,
but the truth—or the lie—
festered.

The anger I carried for Gary Garnett,
the man they called Squeek,
rose up from within me.
It frightened me.

I told my mother:
that if he was not my father,
she should never have told me he was.

I wanted to break something—
because I knew she could never grasp
the weight of the wound,
the depth of my hurt,
or how deeply Gary Garnett revelation scarred me.

Question and Answer Session

My mother gave my brother and me
the chance to ask questions
about our father.

Who knew that day
would be the last time
his name could be spoken aloud—
the last chance to reach
for pieces of Gary Garnett.

We fired questions like a firing squad,
one after another:
Where did you meet?
How long did you date?
Why did you marry?
Why did you divorce?
What was he like?
What was his family like?
Where was he from?

We were nine and ten,
limited by the short reach
of childhood experience.
Our questions danced on the surface
but never broke through.

The question that haunted us most—
the one we could not shape into words—
was simple, searing:
Why did you keep the truth from us?

Do You Want to See Him?

One day, out of the blue,
my mother asked if we wanted to see Gary Garnett.
She never referred to him as our dad—
and neither did we.

His name symbolized pain and division.
Gary Garnett was the hot topic in our household,
but more than him,
we were stunned by what she hid.

When she asked if we wanted to see him,
my brother and I seized the moment.
My mother made the call,
and a meeting was arranged.
The first time, he called to say he couldn't make it.
The second time, he said that he had to work.
The third time, he didn't call at all—
and when my mother tried to speak with him a few days later,
he refused to talk about me and my brother.

Finally, my mother asked,
"Do y'all still want to see him?"

We answered, "No."
I never truly understood,
the weight of that word—
or how deeply it would echo in my life.

Deep Denial

My mother had way of handling pain—
she would deny it away.
Once she did,
it was as if it had never existed.
That is what happen with Gary Garnett.
First, she erased him from her memory.
Every scene where he appeared,
she cut away—
like an editor proofreading a play.
cutting out scenes as she went.

Snip, snip.
"You're out of my life, Gary Garnett."

Deep denial propelled my mother forward.
For better or worse,
it was her coping mechanism.
It helped her survive her most painful experiences,
and Gary Garnett became just another reminder
she refused to face.

But her edits cut into us, too.
I struggled for years to understand who I was.
I would look in a mirror and feel incomplete—
a reflection of only half the person
I was meant to be.

Because of my mother's denial,
I felt she denied me my identity.
It took years, and a lot of therapy,
to make myself whole.

I know she never intended to harm me.
She did the best she could,
carrying her own childhood wounds
into womanhood and motherhood.

Denial was her shield—
and she wielded it with skill.

Deborah
(the mother)
Denial is a temporary solution.

Moving From New Orleans

I moved to Kennedy Heights for peace.
I received it—but in the worst way imaginable.
I ended up on a vacation from reality:
sterile white walls, white lab coats,
the sharp sting of ammonia.

I left New Orleans to find peace.
But the noise only grew louder.
Truths surfaced in my absence.
I needed a fresh start for me and my children:
new scenery, new air, a chance to begin again

We settled into a quaint apartment in Avondale.
My children adjusted quickly—
smiles, laughter, running free.
Their joy depended on me.

But my time with them was cut short.
I was swept away to a mental institution:
sterile white walls, white lab coats,
zombie-like patients shuffling through corridors.

I don't deny I broke.
A bloodied towel where my daughter slept
triggered something fierce inside me:
screaming matches, physical altercations, uncontrollable rage.

The police whisked me away,
to a place I'd known too many times before.
Medications dulled the senses.

Sterile walls closed in.
I left my safe space—my children—behind.
No one explained to them why I was gone.
Their love turned into longing,
confusion, and sadness.

Months later, I clawed my way back home.
I began planning our return to New Orleans—
back to stability, calm, and love.

But the truths waiting there were heavy.
My children were too young to grasp the puzzle:
trauma, psychiatric diagnoses, biological secrets.

The world felt like it was collapsing around me.
I paid dearly for leaving New Orleans.
Instead of healing, it fractured us further.
Family ties severed.
Confusion multiplied.
I regret leaving New Orleans.

Never Tell Them

I never had any intention to tell my children the truth.
I believed the truth would only hurt.
How could I tear away the only father they knew?

So, I told Kelly and T— that June was their dad.
June had raised them—
since Kelly was a baby
and T— was in my belly.

Family pressed me again and again:
"Tell them the truth."
But I refused.

As their mother, I chose what was best for them.
In my heart of hearts, I did what I thought was best.
And I was prepared to go to my grave
believing I had made the right decision.

The truth I buried was this:
Gary "Squeek" Anthony Garnett was their father.
But Arthur "June" Joseph—
the man with no biological ties—
was the only father they knew.
The only one who stayed.

So, I vowed, no matter what,
I would never tell.

Wasn't Their Place

During another breakdown,
while I was away,
my parents stepped in
and took my children.

And while my children were in their care,
my parents told them the truth.

I never knew what they hoped to gain.
All, I know is this—
they harmed my children
more than my silence ever did.

It was never their place
to tell a nine-year-old,
an eight-year-old,
and a five-year-old
that "Squeek" was Kelly and T—'s father.

When I returned home,
there were so much to repair.
So much brokenness to mend.

But one thing remains certain:
it was never my parents' place
to tell them the truth.

Moving Forward

It was hard to move forward,
but it was necessary.
Kelly and T— had learned the truth,
and inside me boiled anger,
irritation,
and a hollow ache I could not name.

"Squeek" belonged to my past.
But now that my children knew his name,
I had no choice but to guide them
toward their future.

Because June was their father—
the one who raised them,
the one who stayed.

And moving forward,
nothing would ever change that truth.

Arthur
The father that built a foundation,
so that legacy could take flight.

Pulling Away

I don't know exactly when the pulling away began.
I can't pinpoint a date,
but I know things changed
the moment the truth was revealed.

When my children found out I wasn't their father...
I started to pull away.

I won't exaggerate.
Deborah and I always fought.
But after the truth,
the fights turned sharper, louder, more violent.

Coincidence? Maybe.
But every argument came back to one name—

Squeek.

I was angry.
Angry that I was losing my children.
I had been there when Kelly was a baby,
and T— was still in Deborah's belly.

I was the one they knew.
And now—
I was being asked to let them go.

They were my children,
and I was the one there for them—
not Squeek.

I was afraid of losing them;
however, I knew they needed to
know Squeek.
I had to push through my fear.
I wanted what was best for my children.
Squeek was their father, but I was their dad.

Gary

The biological father—absent, but never forgotten.
A voice of regret, longing, and quiet truth.

Barbershop Encounter

I walked fast,
head down,
hoping to pass unseen.
But half a block away,
Mr. S— caught me.

I stopped dead in my tracks.

He called my kids over.
I couldn't believe how big they had grown.
No picture could've shown me this.

And then—
he told them, in front of me,

"This is your father."

My heart sank.
T— burst into tears.
I stood frozen,
horrified.

This was not the way.
Not the time.
Not the place.

I had lost them once,
and now I lost the chance
to tell them myself.

School Visit

I see Kelly and my son
playing on the school playground.

Two years since I last laid eyes on them.

I called out,
unsure if they would hear me,
or even recognize me.

They stopped.
Startled.
Confused.

They didn't know me.

They asked how I knew their names.
I couldn't bring myself to say it—
that I was their father.

Then the bell rang.
They said they had to go.

I stood outside the fence,
watching them walk away.

And though they didn't know me,
I felt relief.
At least they seemed happy.

Mother-In-Law's Plan

My ex-mother-in-law invited me to her home.
Kelly and my son were there.
She begged me to come and see them.

I hadn't seen them since they were six and five.
Pictures had once kept me connected.
Then they stopped.
And so did my lifeline.

This time, the visit felt different.
The kids warmed up to me.
It wasn't like before.
For a moment, I believed it could last.

Then, as I rose to leave,
she looked at me and said:

"You can take Kelly and T— home with you."

The words hit like a stone in my chest.
I tried to hide my face.
I wasn't ready.
I wasn't equipped.

And so—
I left without them.

Wedding Guest

My ex-in-laws invite me
to their youngest daughter's wedding.

I am excited—
it had been a long time
since I had seen my children.

The pictures stopped.
So had my only connection.

I wanted to talk to them.
They should know I am their father.
But my nerves betrayed me.

I drank.

It did not help.

I approached my son first.
He turned away.

I turned to Kelly.
She did not ignore me.

When I asked if she knew who I was,
and told her I was her father,
She looked at me and said: "So!"

Then she ran.

Irritated, I stumbled after her.
The alcohol pushed me forward,
but it did not steady me.

She ran toward her brother.
Together, they darted out of reach.
Laughing.
Giggling.

Too Fast.

Too Free.

I gave up.

They seemed amused
that I could not catch them.

And still—
I saw how close they were to one another.
That was the only silver lining of the day.

Kelly
(Adult)
"My legacy is woven by the love of three."

Not My Real Daddy

I was nine
when I learned
June wasn't my real daddy.
Arthur "June" Joseph—
the man who tucked me in,
who taught me to ride a bike—
wasn't the one
who made me.

Ten years later, driving home from New Roads—
before I could speak of it with him.
We were driving home from New Roads,
just the two of us.
I approached the subject reluctantly,
yet I knew this was the moment—
the best time to ask about
Gary Garnett, also called "Squeek."

I believed that, without my mother's presence,
my daddy could be candid.
He lived under the same silence—
the gag order that bound
both me and my brother.

That conversation opened my eyes.
He confessed he had always felt
T— and I deserved to know the truth—
that Squeek was our father.

Even though he disagreed,
he had honored my mother's wishes.

That day, I saw my daddy
in the brightest light—
not as a man bound by blood,
but as one bound by love.

And no matter what,
he would always
be my daddy.

Not His Decision

My daddy said:
"It was never his decision to keep Squeek away."

He believed we should see our father.
He knew the truth would surface one day.
He feared that it would confuse us.

He said it again and again:
It was never his decision.
Not to keep the truth from us.
No to stop us from seeing Squeek.
Not to pretend Squeek didn't exist.
Not to erase the fact that Squeek was our father.

And then, suddenly, a memory made sense—
the day he told me,
"Be nice."

I didn't understand it then.
But those two words carried his truth.
He knew that no matter what,
T— and I needed to know Gary Garnett.

If not through relationship,
then at least through truth.

You Ain't Shit

This is one of the hardest poems I've ever written.
It takes me back to the last time
I spoke to my father—
Gary Garnett.

I didn't know
that call would end our relationship—
forever.

It wasn't jubilant.
It wasn't something to celebrate.
From the start, I should have known—
something was off.

He called sounding sad—
and drunk.
I'd made it a rule never to talk
with anyone inebriated—
but I realized too late.

He told me Uncle Cedric had died.
I felt the ache of never meeting him.
Then came the pressure:
I needed to let him meet our daughters.

It annoyed me.
No one tells me what to do.
Besides—my girls already had a Paw Paw.
Arthur Joseph was the only grandfather they knew.
I wasn't ready to tell them
that their Paw Paw wasn't my father.

Then he began rambling, slurring—
words tangled in grief.
I tried to soothe him,
but my gentleness seemed to trigger rage.
"You hate me," he said.
"I do not," I answered.

What I felt was not hate—
it was indifference.
He accused me of lying.
No one had ever questioned my truth.
His words stung deeper
than his abandonment ever had.

If he had known me,
he would have known I despise lies.
Because at nine years old,
I learned the truth of who I was:
June was not my father.
And my mother—
whom I once admired for her honesty—
had hidden it from me.
From that moment on,
lies ended relationships.
No grace was given.
No forgiveness.

And yet, in that conversation,
he tried to break me:
"You can travel all over the world.
It does not make you better than anyone.
You are not better than me.
You are my child—
and you will be nothing more than that."

Still, he tried to keep me on the line,
hungry for conflict—
the kind he always knew.
But I would not feed it.
I would not give him the war he wanted.

My mother told untruths about my lineage.
My mother hid the truth from me.
He was more caught up in the lies
that were told about me.
I could not have known
that would be the last time
I heard his voice.

For two months,
I called him back.
He never answered.
Eventually, I gave up—
and went on with my life.

Eight years later,
my father died.

But what he left me with
was not his presence,
not his wisdom,
not his love.

What he left me with
was a memory I named:
"You Ain't Shit."

It took me years to heal from that call—
almost longer than it took
to heal from his abandonment.

Piecing Together My Identity

I have not figured it out yet.
But I do not know what hurt more—
the abandonment or the aching search for identity.
To me, they have always been tangled together.
One could not exist without the other.

At nine years old, in a single breath, my life shifted.
The confident, feisty young girl vanished—
replaced by someone angry, insecure, and lost.
It would take years to find my way back.
To find me.

Like the changing stages of life,
I became an actress playing dress-up—
trying on identities tied to DNA
and forged by nurture.

I was living nature vs. nurture in real time.
I couldn't explain it,
but I saw—again and again—
how each theory shaped me.

Like a scientist testing a hypothesis,
I learned to embrace both.
I saw, again and again,
how nurture held the starring role.
Other times,
I could only guess—
when DNA whispered through my bones.
But I was a puzzle with too many missing pieces.

I struggled often.
I memorized answers
to questions that came like clockwork:
"What are you?"

For years, I said I was from New Orleans.
It was a shield.
It kept people from asking more.
And it kept me from searching.

That worked—until I had my own daughters.
The urge to know grew louder.
It refused to be silenced.
I felt the urgency in my bones.

Doctor's visits were the worst.
When asked for my biological father's medical history,
the pain suffocated me.
I felt ashamed—
ashamed that I didn't know,
ashamed that there was no history to give.

Still, I couldn't pull the trigger.
I feared rejection.
I feared abandonment—again.
And I knew that reaching out
might fracture the bond I had with my mother.
She was my constant.
I wasn't willing to lose her.

So I kept concocting answers
to questions that haunted me:
"What are you?"
It took years—
therapy,
reflection,
and finally, the courage to seek out my family.
I had to push past the fear.
I had to ask—Who am I?

And with time, introspection,
and the truth of my lineage,
I found my answer.

I am tenacious,
intelligent,
loving,
funny,
and seriously goofy.
I am shaped by the love of three adults:
Deborah, Arthur, and Gary.
I am the legacy of three.

Forgiveness

I can't pinpoint when I forgave my father.
All I know is—holding on to the pain
was exhausting.

Once I realized how much it was weighing me down,
I let it go.
I forgave him.

And in that moment, I understood:
forgiveness was never about him.
It was making peace
with what he did—
and choosing to move forward.

It was about releasing the hurt,
accepting the disappointments,
and rising above it all.

Forgiveness became
the greatest gift I ever gave myself.

The Death of My Father

My daddy told me that "Squeek" had died.
I paused.
Collected my thoughts.
I did not want my face or body to betray me.

I was sad—
but I did not want my daddy to feel the weight
of the loss I was carrying.

I do not know if it was the finality of death,
or the fact that I was no longer indifferent
to Gary "Squeek" Anthony Garnett—
my father.

In death,
he became what he could not be in life.
In my heart,
he was finally my father.

And in losing him,
I believed I had lost the Garnetts too—
the family I never knew.

I realized in that moment,
I might never fully know myself.

That night,
alone,
I cried myself to sleep.

Therapy

It took me an exceptionally long time
to realize I needed help.

I had buried the pain of abandonment,
the ache of rejection,
so deep inside me
that I tried to eat it away.

But as I began to release the weight,
I saw her—
the hurt nine-year-old child
still trying to make sense
of a father who was never there.

I was angry.
I was wounded.
For years, I believed
I had mastered the rage,
tamed the grief.
But I was only carrying it.

Therapy opened the door.
Therapy gave me a space
safe enough for truth—
a space where I could name my fears
and finally face my pain.

It wasn't that I had no understanding
of my childhood trauma—
I did.

It was that I had not recognized
how tightly I was gripping
the baggage of being abandoned,
the weight of being rejected.

In therapy, I regained my voice.
In therapy, I let go.
In therapy, I allowed myself to weep.
And in therapy, I found me.

Finding Myself

The first step to recovery
is admitting you have a problem.
But like many addicts,
I could not admit
I was trauma-bonded
to my parents' choices.

Recovery was long.
Arduous.
Because I couldn't face the truth—
that the pain
had shattered my heart into pieces.

It ran deep.
Touched every part of me.
I was angry at everything
and nothing.

I couldn't explain
how I felt inside.
Words failed me—
because the protection
was the true deception.

Like a fungus in the dark,
the lies grew.
Secrets were kept.
They were nurtured
with more deception—
beguiling the young and innocent.

They stole what was mine from birth:
my identity.

Healing began
when I finally admitted
the pain my parents' decisions caused me.

They robbed me of my truth.
And that angered me
more than anything else.

My identity was rewritten
with their lies.
They erased who I was
and replaced it
with who they wanted me to pretend to be.

Before I could talk,
before I could walk,
I learned to act.
I became
who they told me I was.

In crafting their lies,
I felt a disconnection from my life—
a void I couldn't name.
So I began to fill in the pieces.
I created my own identity.

It kept me going.
Fueled me.
Until I had my own children.

Then, the identity I'd built
began to crumble.
As my daughters grew,
so did my curiosity—
about me.

My rewritten history
wasn't enough
to answer my own questions.

After decades of wondering,
I acted on faith.
I became the investigator
of my own life.

I went to the source—
my paternal family,
and what I found
was healing—
for me,
and for them.

"In that moment,
I felt whole—
not awkward.
I belonged.
And that was the missing piece—
in their lives,
and mine."

I found unconditional love.
I found belonging.

Reconnection

There were so many losses
before the reconnection could be imagined.

2000—my mother passed.
2004—my biological father journeyed on.
2005—my father died.
That same year, relationships unraveled.
2005—mid-year we moved to Sasebo, Japan.

In just five years,
my world was unrecognizable.
Grief clung to me like fog.
I moved through days
like a ghost of myself.

I was a shell—
hollowed by relentless pain.
Disconnected from everyone.
From everything.
From me.

I do not know how I survived.
Then—quietly,
without ceremony—
Something shifted.
I began to reconnect—
to my life,
to my loved ones,
to my purpose.

Hope flickered.
Love returned.
I began to feel again.

Reconnection came
because I had lost so much.
It helped me rediscover
what I thought was gone forever.
The ache had softened.

I was no longer going through the motions.
I was alive.

Reconnection became my rhythm—
one step at a time,
like a child learning to walk.
I was hungry for possibility.
Where would this movement take me?
There was an awakening in me.
I was ready.

Ready to answer
all the questions
I had once been too afraid to ask.

Garnett Family Reunion

I have always felt awkward
in a room full of people.
Family or strangers,
it never mattered—
social spaces unsettled me.

So, I went to the reunion
with no expectations.
I would sit back,
smile when needed,
and quietly pass the time.

But what I found
was something I had never known.
I felt like a queen holding court—
surrounded, celebrated, seen.
Love wrapped itself around me,
and for the first time,
I belonged.

I saw reflections of myself everywhere:
fair complexions,
green eyes, brown eyes, gray eyes,
hair that was curly, hair that was wavy,
hair that was long, hair that was shiny—
faces carrying pieces of me.

In their presence,
awkwardness melted away.
I did not shrink.
I did not hide.
I opened myself to the moment,
and it was the best reunion of my life.

In that space,
I found myself.
I was with my family.
I was loved.

My Teedies

My aunts.
June.
Darnell.
My Teedies—
remarkable women.

Hardworking.
Independent.
Brilliant.
Audaciously funny.

Family historians.
Keepers of the story.
They preserved it,
passed it on,
made sure I knew
where I came from.

In their memories,
I discovered myself—
like a character in a book,
written into the margins,
bound by love.

Acceptance

Nothing is like the grace of acceptance—
the freedom of being seen
for who you are.

To know you belong,
without question,
to a family.

Outside my immediate circle,
I had never known that feeling.

When I reconnected with the Garnetts,
it was as if the heavens opened.
Questions that had lingered
found their voice.
I was loved.
I was claimed.
I was wanted.
I was accepted.

In their embrace,
a socially awkward woman
found herself.
Found her place.
Found where she belonged.

Yes, I will always be awkward.
But I have my people.
I have my place.
And that has made—
all the difference.

Love reached for me—
and I reached back.

Full Circle

After years of therapy,
after seasons of growth,
I have come full circle.

It took me decades,
but time no longer matters.
If there is breath in the body,
there is still room to amend,
to set new goals,
to chart a new course—
even if it means correcting the old one.

I came full circle,
when I acknowledged
the moment that changed everything:
at nine years old,
learning I was not bound to my father
by blood.

At forty-nine,
I finally held the tools
to answer questions
that had lived inside me for a lifetime:
Who am I?
Where do I belong?
Who do I belong to?
Whose face do I carry?
Where did these green eyes come from?
This skin so light?
Why did pictures feel awkward?
Why did I feel foreign
in my own skin?
I was no longer afraid of the answers.
All my questions circled back
to one man—
my father,
Gary Anthony "Squeek" Garnett.
The missing link.
Silently, I wondered:
How much of him lives in me?

When I found the strength
to face the truth,
I was closer to closing the circle.

When I received the answers,
the circle was complete.
I had finally—
come full circle.

Healing My Heart

There was always this nagging feeling,
lurking in the shadows,
appearing and reappearing
at the most inopportune times.

It stalked me,
cornered me,
until I was forced
to take stock of myself
and call it by name.

Throughout my life,
it wore many names:
Abandonment.
Disappointment.
Rejection.

I told myself
I was managing well—
that I could bury my sadness,
contain my anger.

But in truth,
the feelings I refused to name
rose up in exhaustion—
too tired to push back,
too heavy to suppress.

Pain pressed down:
abandonment,
rejection.

Years passed in retrospection,
introspection,
over-analysis.
I kept pushing the feelings away.

Until one day,
my heart and mind
stood in one accord.

No longer denying,
I faced the truth.

The nine-year-old inside me
picked up the broken pieces
and whispered what I had never wanted to acknowledge:
Arthur "June" Joseph Jr.
was not my father.
Gary "Squeek" Garnett
was.

At nine years old,
I lost both fathers—
the one who raised me,
and the one who gave me life.
My world was never the same.
I coped the way a child does:
pretending Gary Garnett never existed,
clinging to my mother,
watching my father
pull away from my brother and me.

I buried my pain.
I smiled through it.
And as I grew older,
I ate my sorrow away.
Still pretending.
Still hurting.

Then—
an epiphany:
to make peace
with what no longer served me.
It began with forgiveness.
And slowly,
anger dissolved.
Disappointment softened.
My heart began to heal.

The nine-year-old girl,
reconciled
with the forty-something woman.

For the first time,
I allowed myself to cry.
Not deny.
Not push away.

I cried for my father,
Gary Anthony "Squeek" Garnett.
And this time,
I did not stop the tears.
As they washed over me,
they carried the pain away.
And in their flow,
my heart—
finally healed.

About the Author

Kelly Garnett Joseph-Brooks was born and raised in New Orleans, Louisiana, where storytelling, rhythm, and resilience sparked her earliest creative flames. A writer, creative educator, and exceptional speaker, Kelly began journaling and writing poetry to capture her imagination and process the world around her. It has been her saving grace.

In 2002, she became an educator, earning credentials in Special Education, English as a Second Language (ESL), and Generalist teaching. Her classroom became a space of transformation, where writing and journaling helped students heal, reflect, and grow into lifelong learners.

Though Kelly retired from teaching in 2018, she remains an educator at heart. Her essence is rooted in guiding others—believing that knowledge is the light that moves us forward and strengthens our communities.

Her first poetry collection was born from the pages of her journal, where she discovered that her words were more than prose—they were echoes of her heart. Each poem became a pathway to healing, written to encourage others to find healthy ways to navigate trauma, disappointment, and uncertainty.

During the COVID-19 pandemic, Kelly penned *Dreaming Beyond: Finding My Voice and Keeping My Sanity During the COVID-19 Pandemic*, a poetry collection that explores healing, emotion, and personal truth. Her poetry chapbook *Inheritance: A Journey in Three Movements* is also scheduled for release in 2025. She is currently editing her second poetry collection, continuing her exploration of healing, voice, and personal truth.

Kelly is also the author of three children's books, each scheduled for release in 2026:

• *Please Bring Your Monster to Camp*
• *Please Bring Your Monster to Yoga Class*
• *Marley the Monster*

Her work celebrates emotional truth, honors the power of voice, and highlights the rhythm of healing and storytelling. Whether writing for children or adults, Kelly's words invite readers to reflect, laugh, and grow. *Yes, indeed.*

"When I began to write,
my voice mirrored my yearning for peace."

Kelly Garnett Joseph-Brooks—

Final Whisper: Echoes Beyond the Page

Healing is not a destination.
It is the quiet unfolding of truth,
one poem at a time.

Three voices shaped my story,
but only mine could set it free.

Sección Bilingüe/Bilingual Section

Table of Contents/Tabla de Contenidos

Introduccion
Un Sueño en Dos Idiomas/A Dream in Two Languages   1

Fundamentos Destrozados/Shattered Foundations   5

Sanando Mi Corazon/Healing My Heart   7

Mi Verdad Comienza Aqui/My Truth Begins Here   9

Encontrandome a Mi Misma/Finding Myself   11

Alejandome/Pulling Away   13

La Muerte de Mi Padre/The Death of My Father   16

Kelly, Adelante/Kelly, Move Forward   18

Lecciones Tácitas/Unspoken Lessons   22

Final Page Flourish
Legado en Dos Idiomas: Adelante, Poeta.   25

Un Sueño en Dos Idiomas

Mi segunda colección de poesía me ha dado tiempo para reflexionar, hacer las paces con el pasado y avanzar hacia el futuro. Al hacerlo, recordé los sueños de una niña—mis primeros recuerdos de soñar en voz alta. Compartí esos sueños con mi madre. Ella escuchaba con atención, me animaba y me recordaba suavemente esos sueños en diferentes etapas de mi vida. Hacía lo que hacía excepcionalmente bien: me impulsaba hacia adelante.

Uno de los sueños más vívidos que tuve fue aprender a hablar varios idiomas. Decidí comenzar con el español. Mis dos años de español en la Universidad de Houston (¡Go Coogs!) me dieron una base sólida. Mi meta es hablar español con fluidez cuando viajemos a la República Dominicana. Mi objetivo final es mudarme allí y ofrecerme como voluntaria en la comunidad, utilizando mis amplias habilidades como educadora.

Esta sección bilingüe es un puente—entre el inglés y el español, entre el pasado y el futuro, entre los sueños de una niña y el espíritu de la madre que creyó en ella. Es mi forma de reconectar, reclamar y avanzar.

A Dream in Two Languages☐

My second poetry collection has given me time to reflect, make peace with the past, and move forward toward my future. In doing so, I remembered the dreams of a young girl—my earliest memories of dreaming out loud. I shared those dreams with my mother. She would listen attentively, encourage me, and gently remind me of those dreams at different stages of my life. She did what she did exceptionally well: she pushed me forward.

One of the most vivid dreams I had was to learn to speak several languages. I decided to begin with Spanish. My two years of Spanish at the University of Houston (Go Coogs!) gave me a strong foundation. My goal is to speak Spanish fluently when we travel to the Dominican Republic. Ultimately, I hope to move there and volunteer in the community, using my extensive skills as an educator.

This bilingual section is a bridge—between English and Spanish, between past and future, between the dreams of a young girl and the spirit of the mother who believed in her. It is my way of reconnecting, reclaiming, and reaching forward.

Poemas en Español

Fundamentos Destrozados

Fundamentos Destrozados

Era un sábado cualquiera,
pero para nosotros—los Tres Mosqueteros intrépidos—
era una aventura con el abuelo.
Vivíamos con nuestros abuelos,
porque mamá estaba de vacaciones de la realidad
y papá no podía cuidarnos.

Nos vestimos con emoción,
sin saber que ese día
sería el comienzo de una grieta
que nunca dejaría de expandirse.

Avondale, Louisiana,
se sentía como tierra extranjera.
Yo era una visitante en mi propia historia,
una niña buscando sentido
en medio de adultos que hablaban en claves.

Fue allí donde conocí la tristeza,
no como una palabra,
sino como una sombra que se sentaba a mi lado.
Mi primer roce con la depresión
no vino con lágrimas,
sino con silencio.

Sanando Mi Corazón

Sanando Mi Corazón

Durante años,
guardé sentimientos que no podía nombrar.
Abandono, decepción, rechazo—
palabras que dolían más cuando se quedaban en silencio.

Intenté entender por qué
mi corazón se rompía cada vez que pensaba en él.
Arthur Joseph Jr.
era un nombre que llevaba como una sombra,
pero nunca se sintió como hogar.

Me preguntaba si el dolor era mío,
o si lo había heredado
como una maleta llena de secretos.
Finalmente,
dejé de buscar respuestas en los lugares equivocados.
Miré dentro de mí,
y encontré la verdad que siempre había estado allí.
Gary "Squeek" Garnett
no era solo un recuerdo—
era mi padre.
Y en ese reconocimiento,
comenzó la sanación.

Mi Verdad Comienza Aquí

Mi Verdad Comienza Aquí

Tenía nueve años
cuando el mundo dejó de sentirse seguro.
Arthur "June" Joseph
no era mi padre,
pero durante años,
su nombre fue una mentira que me envolvía.

Papá no estaba allí,
y el silencio se convirtió en mi compañía.
Aprendí a leer miradas,
a escuchar lo que no se decía.

La confusión se convirtió en identidad,
y la identidad en una herida sin nombre.
Me preguntaba si la culpa era mía,
si el abandono era algo que merecía.

Pero la poesía me encontró.
Me dio palabras
cuando el mundo me ofrecía silencio.
Me dio fuerza
cuando la verdad dolía demasiado para decirla en voz alta.

Hoy rompo el ciclo.
Hoy reclamo mi historia.
Mi verdad comienza aquí—
con cada verso,
con cada lágrima convertida en luz.

Encontrándome a Mí Misma

Encontrándome a Mí Misma

Durante años,
me dijeron quién era
sin preguntarme cómo me sentía.
Me enseñaron a sonreír
cuando el dolor me ahogaba por dentro.
La verdad era difícil de admitir.
No porque no la supiera,
sino porque decirla
significaba romper el silencio
que otros habían construido para mí.

Me tomó tiempo sanar,
tiempo para entender
que el amor no debería doler,
que la identidad no se impone.

Las mentiras me hicieron dudar,
los secretos me hicieron pequeña.
Pero la poesía me dio espacio
para respirar,
para gritar sin miedo.

Hoy me encuentro a mí misma
en cada verso,
en cada verdad que ya no escondo.
No soy lo que me dijeron que era.
Soy lo que elegí ser.

Alejándome

Alejándome

No sé exactamente cuándo comenzó el alejamiento.
No puedo señalar una fecha,
pero sé que todo cambió
en el momento en que se reveló la verdad.

Cuando mis hijos descubrieron que no era su padre…
empecé a alejarme.

No voy a exagerar.
Deborah y yo siempre discutíamos.
Pero después de la verdad,
las peleas se volvieron más agudas, más fuertes, más violentas.

¿Coincidencia? Tal vez.
Pero cada discusión volvía a un solo nombre—

Squeek.

Estaba enojado.
Enojado porque estaba perdiendo a mis hijos.
Yo estuve allí cuando Kelly era un bebé,
y T— aún estaba en el vientre de Deborah.

Yo era el que ellos conocían.
Y ahora—
me pedían que los dejara ir.

Eran mis hijos,
y yo fui quien estuvo allí para ellos—
no Squeek.

Tenía miedo de perderlos;
sin embargo, sabía que necesitaban
conocer a Squeek.

Tuve que superar mi miedo.
Quería lo mejor para mis hijos.
Squeek era su padre, pero yo era su papá.

La Muerte de Mi Padre

La Muerte de Mi Padre

Me lo dijo Squeek:
"Tu padre murió."
Y aunque sabía que algo estaba mal,
no estaba preparada para esa verdad.

Sentí tristeza,
pero también confusión.
¿Cómo llorar a alguien
que siempre estuvo lejos?

Intenté recordar momentos,
pero la distancia era más fuerte que los recuerdos.
No sabía si lloraba por él,
o por lo que nunca tuvimos.

Me sentí sola.
No por su ausencia,
sino por la ausencia de conexión.

La muerte llegó sin reconciliación,
sin palabras finales,
sin abrazos que cerraran heridas.

Y aún así,
algo dentro de mí se rompió.
No por lo que fue,
sino por lo que nunca pudo ser.

Kelly Adelante

Kelly, Adelante

Antes creía que avanzar
era la forma de sobrellevar la decepción,
la tristeza y el dolor.

Sin importar lo que pasara,
me levantaba,
me sacudía el polvo
y seguía adelante.

Pero nunca me di tiempo para detenerme—
para procesar,
para liberar.

No estaba avanzando.
Estaba huyendo.

Cuando dejé de huir,
empecé a procesar y liberar.

Ahora, cuando avanzo,
lo hago con intención.

Avanzo como la mejor versión de mí misma.
Ya no huyo de la decepción, la tristeza ni el dolor.

Avanzar es mi nuevo mantra.
Me ayuda a reconocer
la decepción, la tristeza y el dolor.
Ahora, cuando me levanto,
me sacudo el polvo
y avanzo,
lo hago con intención y propósito.
Ahora entiendo lo que significa avanzar—
reconciliar la versión rota

con la nueva versión de mí.

Kelly, Adelante.

Kelly, Move Forward

I thought moving forward
helped one to deal with disappointment,
sadness, and pain.

No matter what happened,
I would pick myself up,
dust myself off and move forward.
I never made any time to stop,
process, and release.
I was not moving forward—
I was running.
When I stopped running,
I began to process and release.
So now when I move forward,
I move with intentionality.

I move forward as the best version of myself.
I no longer run from disappoint, sadness, and pain.

Moving forward is my new mantra.
It helps me to acknowledge disappointment,
sadness and pain.

Now, when I pick myself up, dust myself off, and move forward,
I move with intentionality and purpose.
I now know what it means to move forward.

Reconciling the broken you—with the new version of yourself.

Kelly, Move Forward.

Lecciones Tácitas

Lecciones Tácitas

Guardar secretos puede dañar un legado,
fracturar los lazos familiares,
crear confusión,
provocar incertidumbre,
fomentar tristeza,
erosionar la confianza,
y dejar atrás enojo y retraimiento.

Pero cuando se honra la verdad,
se comprende el legado,
se amplía la visión de la familia,
se prepara el corazón para información que cambia la vida,
se brinda apoyo parental,
se involucra a un terapeuta si es necesario,
se protege del dolor,
se fortalece la confianza,
y se crea alegría y amor para compartir.

Unspoken Lessons

Secrets mar (damage) legacies,
fractures family bonds,
creates confusion,
leads to uncertainty,
fosters sadness,
erodes trust,
and leaves behind anger and withdrawal.

When truth is honored,
understands legacy,
expands understanding of family,
prepares for life changing information,
provides parental support,
involves a therapist (if necessary),
protects from sadness,
increases trust,
and creates joy and love to share.

Final Page Flourish □
Legado en Dos Idiomas: Adelante, Poeta.

Legado en Dos Idiomas: Adelante, Poeta.

Mi legado bilingüe florece sin fin, con fuerza—
un susurro que se convierte en verso,
una promesa que danza entre dos mundos,
y un verso que nunca termina;
sobrevivió al silencio y canta a los cielos.

☐ *Como una pluma en el aire,*
mis poemas cruzan aguas y fronteras—
uniendo inglés y español en un vuelo de verdad y belleza.

Legacy in Two Languages: Move Forward, Poet.

My bilingual legacy blooms endlessly with strength—
a whisper that becomes verse,
a promise that dances between two worlds,
and a verse that never ends;
it survived silence and sings to the heavens.

Like a feather in the air,
my poems cross waters and borders—
uniting English and Spanish in a flight of truth and beauty.

www.ingramcontent.com/pod-product-compliance
Lightning Source LLC
LaVergne TN
LVHW041230080426
835508LV00011B/1134